CROSS-EXAMINED

Also by Josh Scott:

Bible Stories for Grown-Ups:
Reading Scripture with New Eyes

Context:
Putting Scripture in Its Place

Parables:
Putting Jesus's Stories in Their Place

Learn more about Josh Scott
and his books at
AbingdonPress.com/josh_scott

Josh Scott

Racism

CROSS-EXAMINED

Reading the Bible in Times of Division

Gender equality

LGBTQ+ inclusion

Weaponizing the Bible

Christian Nationalism

Abingdon Press | Nashville

Cross-Examined

Reading the Bible in Times of Division

Library of Congress Control Number: 2025932879
ISBN 978-1-7910-3937-0

MANUFACTURED IN THE
UNITED STATES OF AMERICA

Contents

Download a FREE Discussion Guide for *Cross-Examined.*

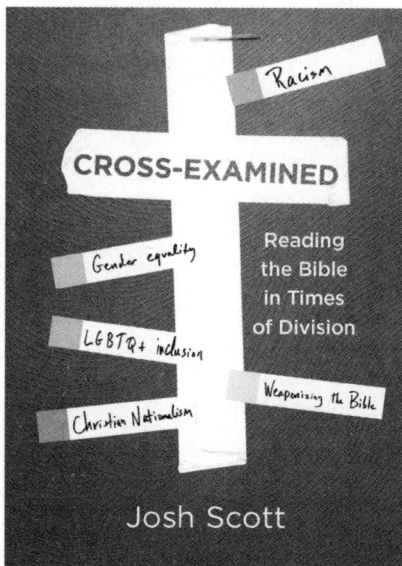

CROSS-EXAMINED

Racism

Gender equality

LGBTQ+ inclusion

Christian Nationalism

Weaponizing the Bible

Reading
the Bible
in Times
of Division

Josh Scott

Scan the QR code on the right or visit **https://formtitan.com /s/w2lq** to download.

Introduction

My current obsession is true crime podcasts. Anyone else? My week is punctuated by the anticipation of the next episode of *Crime Junkie*, *The Prosecutors*, or *Big Mad True Crime*. I know it can seem weird, especially for people who aren't into true crime. My only defense is that it really isn't my fault. When I was a kid, my mom watched shows like *Perry Mason* and *Matlock*, and I ended up getting engrossed in those stories too.

Something happens in every courtroom whodunit, regardless of the show. If you pay attention, there's a template that each one seems to follow. A crime has occurred, usually a murder, and someone has been arrested and will have to stand trial. What we know, as viewers, is that the person being tried didn't really do it. We know, somehow, that they are innocent, if only because we trust the intuition and integrity of Ben Matlock and Perry Mason. However, even with that hunch, the case isn't looking good. It seems inevitable that the wrong person is going to be found guilty and the real culprit will go free.

But not so fast! Just when it seems like the defendant is done for, then comes the final cross-examination. In that moment, the titular character unveils previously unheard or unknown information, and it changes the case. Their innocence is proved, the guilty party is nabbed, and all is right with the world. All, mind you, in the span of about sixty minutes.

This book hopes to do something similar with beliefs, cross-examining them, questioning them in order to put the truth out in the open. Many of us have inherited understandings of really important things—like the Bible, theology, and faith—that seem airtight. These interpretations then become embedded in our worldview, and we are even implicitly taught that to question them is to question God. That was true for me. I was given an understanding of the Bible that led to a particular set of beliefs about the topics we will explore in the pages ahead. For the first two decades of my life, those interpretations made sense and went largely unquestioned; those interpretations worked for me. Well, that is, until they didn't. As I began to see the real, human impact of my theology and interpretations, I could not help but cross-examine these ideas. What I discovered was that I was given *an* interpretation but not the *only* interpretation. There were other Christians who read and interpreted the texts and our theological tradition differently.

That led me on a journey to cross-examine each of the important topics in this book, and the more I learned about the context of the Bible and the development of our tradition, the more I became convinced—perhaps convicted is a better word—that the exclusive, exclusionary, and narrow interpretations I had been handed did not do the text, tradition, God, or people justice.

This book will invite you into that experience of cross-examining the dominant interpretations and understandings of key issues that all play a crucial role in determining what the future of Christianity in America (and perhaps beyond) will be. As we explore the ways Scripture has been weaponized, women have been limited in their roles in the church, how our LGBTQ+ siblings have been excluded, and how racism and Christian nationalism have distorted our understanding of God and humanity, an alternative understanding will emerge. For me, this understanding has been transformative, and the previous interpretations I inherited could not withstand that cross-examination.

There is a chance that some readers have already made the journey that will unfold in these pages, and you are looking for a resource to help you talk about these important ideas with others. I think you'll find that here. While not exhaustive by any stretch of the imagination, the treatment of these topics will serve as a good introduction to some vitally important conversations and offer ways to (re)think about them.

For others, perhaps you are coming to this little volume to learn brand new information. Maybe you're even reading this reluctantly, at the behest of someone you love who is trying to explain the journey they are experiencing. First, let me say thank you. Even reading these words is an act of love and care. Second, let me invite you to enter this conversation with an open mind and heart. I am confident that my love and compassion are far exceeded by God's. We are not trying to make God nicer or improve God's image. God is love, and because of that, God has always been out in front of us calling us forward. God is leading us to a more just and generous humanity, and not the other way around.

What lies ahead takes the Bible, the tradition, and our faith very seriously. My guess is you do too. Let's lean into this conversation together with openness and a hopeful sense of possibility. The cross-examination begins now.

1

Weaponizing the Bible

In 2004, MGM released a film called *Saved!* a satirical comedy focused on evangelical culture. Needless to say, the film was met with mixed reactions, especially among the group being satirized, a group to which I belonged at the time. I was probably in the minority, but I thought the film was good—funny, challenging, even smart. More than that, it rang true to my own experience, which I had begun to question at the time.

In one particular scene, the central characters experience a dramatic conflict that encapsulates so much of the entire film. Let me set it up briefly. The central plot of the movie revolves around Mary, a teenage girl who discovers that she is pregnant, all the while attending an evangelical Christian school. While at this point the pregnancy is unknown to anyone else, Hilary Faye, the most popular and (self) righteous student at the school, senses something shifting with Mary. The only solution, Hilary Faye decides, is to stage not an intervention but an exorcism. As you might expect, Mary doesn't want to participate, which leads to the following interaction.

> HILARY FAYE: Mary, turn away from Satan. Jesus, he loves you.

> MARY: You don't know the first thing about love.

> HILARY FAYE, *throwing a Bible at Mary*: I am *filled* with Christ's love! You are just jealous of my success in the Lord!

> MARY, *holding up the Bible:* This is not a weapon! You idiot!

Yes, the scene is over the top and extreme; that's satire for you. Most Christians don't throw Bibles at other people. However, it also speaks to a real problem that we cannot ignore. The Bible is far too often used as a weapon. While physical copies of Scripture are not being chucked around, the contents of the Bible are used by some to shame, exclude, and harm those who don't fall into whatever version of orthodoxy is being used as a litmus test.

In my role as a pastor, it is almost daily—and that is not an exaggeration—that I talk to someone who has been on the receiving end of the Bible's weaponization. Generally, these dear humans who fashion a weapon from the text are not people who hate the Bible. In fact, often they are folks who grew up with the Bible and have loved the Bible so much they studied it intently, even memorizing large chunks of it. When I talk to them, the grief and pain they have experienced are palpable. There's a feeling of betrayal, for sure, but what always stands out to me is the grief and sense of loss. They feel the Bible has been taken from them only to be turned around and used against them. Perhaps the most unbearable fact of all is that most of the people I talk to, even after being victimized by the quoting of Scripture, still grieve the loss of the Bible. They do not hate Scripture even now; as exiled and estranged as they might feel, they still miss the Bible.

All that leads me to ask a series of important questions: How can words of life, hope, and healing be used to inflict such pain, despair, and wounding? What causes people who would ordinarily be kind and compassionate to flip a switch and start doing the verbal and emotional equivalent of throwing a Bible at others? In short, how did we get here, and is there anything we can do about it?

You might ask what weaponizing the Bible looks like practically if it's usually not an actual Bible being thrown at someone. The Bible is weaponized anytime it is quoted and used to limit, exclude, and malign the flourishing of any God's children. Some followers of Jesus are drawn to the idea of seeing Scripture as a sword (Ephesians 6:17) to use on others, instead of a scalpel intended to perform needed surgery on our own hearts (Hebrews 4:12). Both images are in Scripture, and we must decide which leads to a more Christlike approach to the Bible.

I'll introduce a few examples that we will explore in more depth in the rest of this book. To begin with, people weaponize the Bible against women by ignoring texts that affirm the leadership capabilities and equality of women, opting for texts that seek to diminish and silence their voices and contributions.

I vividly remember hearing a woman in one church being told that she was not allowed to share her perspective on a particular issue because of 1 Timothy 2:

> Let a woman learn in silence with full submission. I do not permit a woman to teach or to have authority over a man; she is to keep silent. For Adam was formed first, then Eve, and Adam was not deceived, but the woman was deceived and became a transgressor.
>
> (1 Timothy 2:11-14)

Just think about how much the Christian tradition has lost and missed by not listening to the voices of women, who bear God's image just as fully as men.

We can also see the same pattern in how many Christians view the LGBTQ+ community. Some quote texts that seem to call homosexuality sinful ("seem" being the key word here) while ignoring other texts that refute their interpretations. These segments of the Bible, often called "clobber passages," are quoted in order to condemn and deny belonging to others. Texts like Leviticus 18:22 and Romans 1:26-27 are often referenced to prove that LGBTQ+ people are "sinful" and "unnatural."

> *You shall not lie with a male as with a woman; it is an abomination.*
>
> (*Leviticus 18:22*)

> *For this reason God gave them over to dishonorable passions. Their females exchanged natural intercourse for unnatural, and in the same way also the males, giving up natural intercourse with females, were consumed with their passionate desires for one another. Males committed shameless acts with males and received in their own persons the due penalty for their error.*
>
> (*Romans 1:26-27*)

Sadly, the church has brought so much harm to our LGBTQ+ siblings, who long to participate fully in the life and ministry of the church but have been largely denied by the vast majority of churches and denominations. They have also experienced hate, bigotry, and vitriol from pastors in pulpits and congregants in pews. The weaponization against this community has garnered a literal body count and is not grounded in divine will but human bias.

Further, people have cited Scripture as a source of legitimation for racism, xenophobia, and nationalism. The Bible has been cited and quoted to excuse slavery, segregation, and injustice against non-white people, ranging from the treatment of the Native peoples of North America to the Atlantic slave trade to the vilification and mistreatment of immigrants and more, people have found a chapter and verse to support all kinds of heinous behavior toward those they deem outsiders. Texts like Genesis 4:15 and 9:25, respectively focused on the "mark of Cain" and the "curse of Ham," have been distorted and twisted to excuse the mistreatment and justify the inequality of non-white people. Sometimes, this practice is referred to as *prooftexting*, which means using specific Bible passages to support a position, often without regard for the fuller historical and literary context of the biblical book being invoked.

These texts and others are combined and then come to expression in the kind of Christian nationalism that is sweeping the United States as I write these words. Some readers of the Bible conclude that texts like Matthew 28, known as the Great Commission, give them cover to spew misinformation and hate, force others to accept their specific understanding of Christianity, all while they seek to turn their misinterpretations into law.

A brief disclaimer is in order before we continue. I have been on both sides of this conversation. Thirty years ago, I was a high school student who read the Bible compulsively and took the random verses I found that seemed applicable as calling out the "sin" of a friend or classmate. Today, I am a pastor providing care to those who are recipients of the same kind of irresponsible approach to the Bible. From this experience, as both a weaponizer of Scripture and now as someone who seeks to deweaponize it, I have learned that this conversation comes down to our understanding of the Bible—both where it comes from and what it actually is.

Growing up, I had no frame of reference for these questions. From where or from whom did the Bible originate? As a kid I just assumed that the Bible was somehow dropped from the sky, leather-bound and with gilded edges, my name embossed on the cover, and in the King James Version, of course. Our position was that if the KJV was good enough for Jesus and Paul, then it was good enough for us. I had no idea, no frame of reference for the fact that the world and people that produced the Bible were not my own, or that the Bible was a process, not a product of one particular time, place, or author. In this instance, fact is far more interesting than fiction. To put it succinctly, the Bible did not parachute down from the heavens. It is the product of real people living in real contexts, and what they wrote was significantly shaped by when and where they lived.

To begin with, the Bible is not a book; it is a library. The very meaning of the Greek word *biblia*, from which we get the English word *Bible*, means "books." That's plural. Not one book, but books. Like me, you might be surprised to learn that there is more than one version of this library. Many of us are familiar with the Protestant canon that includes sixty-six books—thirty-nine in the Old Testament and twenty-seven in the New. *Canon* here comes from the Greek meaning "rule" or "measuring stick" and is used to refer to texts that have been understood to have authority.

What might not be as familiar is the fact that not every Christian group or tradition has the same collection of sacred texts. For example, if we were to peruse a Catholic version of the Bible, we would find those same sixty-six books, with an additional seven books known as the *deuterocanonical texts* (which means "second canon"). These are books that were part of the Greek translation of the Hebrew Bible, called the *Septuagint*, but are not part of the Hebrew Bible or the Protestant canon. When Catholics talk about the Bible, they are referencing this canon, which contains seventy-three books, not only the sixty-six known to Protestants. But it doesn't end there. The Ethiopian and Eritrean Orthodox Churches have more than eighty books in their canon. This means that when someone says "the Bible," it means different things to different groups of people.

Further, the Bible was written over a period of around one thousand years. Think about how much has changed in America in our less than 250 years as a country. We could even limit that conversation to the last decade, and we'd still have a lot to talk about! Now imagine the process of the Bible, written over a thousand-year period (roughly from 1000 BCE to 125 CE) and referring to events that are even further in the past. This means the Bible doesn't have *a* context (singular) but contexts (plural). It was written under the rule of multiple, successive empires that each had their own unique impact on Israel, Judah, and the early Christian community, respectively—Assyria, Babylon, Persia, Greece, and Rome all played a major role in the development of these texts.

Additionally, if the Bible is a library, and I believe it is, then that must play a role in how we understand what it is and how it should be engaged. While not as popular as they were in the past, how many of us have ever benefited from the use of a public library? Probably most of us, right? Have you ever walked into a public library expecting uniformity, that all the books in that library would be from the same author, time period, genre, or perspective? Of course not. Libraries are diverse, and the Bible as a library is too. The collection of texts in a library reflects the growth and change of our understanding over time, and so does the Bible.

A couple of examples of this might be helpful here. First, notice this passage from Deuteronomy, which focuses on generational sin:

> *I the LORD your God am a jealous God, punishing children for the iniquity of parents to the third and fourth generation of those who reject me but showing steadfast love to the thousandth generation of those who love me and keep my commandments.*
> *(Deuteronomy 5:9-10)*

The meaning here is plain. In the understanding of this author, God will punish children for the sins of their parents for as many as three or four generations. This reflects the idea of generational curses, that children and grandchildren and great-grandchildren can and will be held responsible for their parents' sins. That, however, is not the perspective of the entirety of Scripture. Notice this passage from the prophet Ezekiel, which offers a markedly different understanding than Deuteronomy:

> The word of the LORD came to me: What do you mean by repeating this proverb concerning the land of Israel, "The parents have eaten sour grapes, and the children's teeth are set on edge"? As I live, says the Lord GOD, this proverb shall no more be used by you in Israel. Know that all lives are mine; the life of the parent as well as the life of the child is mine: it is only the person who sins who shall die.
>
> (Ezekiel 18:1-4)

Between Deuteronomy and Ezekiel, a renegotiation had occurred. The perspective had shifted, grown. The prophet breaks with the previous understanding and instead suggests that humans are accountable for their own actions, not bound to the failures of those who came before them. Generational curses aren't binding or even real, according to Ezekiel.

This is not a one-off, isolated incident in the Bible. We find these kinds of shifts again and again. Are Moabites evil and to be excluded as the author of Deuteronomy suggests, or can they be a hero like Ruth, who saves the day? Does God want us to beat our plowshares into swords, as Joel believes, or does the position of Isaiah reflect God's dream of a world free from violence, with swords beaten into plowshares?

The Bible, written over such a long period of time, reflects the conversations, challenges, and questions of our ancient spiritual ancestors. Over time, as they learned new things about God, humanity, and the world, they adjusted their interpretations to make space for the new truths they were learning. Like us, the authors of the biblical texts and the communities they belonged to were in process. They didn't just get all the information they needed downloaded to their brains by God in an instant. God worked with them, invited and led them over time as they had the capacity.

This reality is even attested to in Scripture itself in the Gospel of John as Jesus's ministry is reaching its crescendo. The confrontation and collision between his kingdom of God vision and a Roman cross was imminent. In chapters 14–17 Jesus offers his Farewell Discourse, a series of teachings to prepare the disciples for his impending departure. In chapter 16 he begins to describe to his disciples the work of the Spirit, who would be sent to guide and comfort them in his absence.

> *"I still have many things to say to you, but you cannot bear them now. When the Spirit of truth comes, he will guide you into all the truth, for he will not speak on his own but will speak whatever he hears, and he will declare to you the things that are to come."*
> *(John 16:12-13)*

Notice that Jesus doesn't tell them they've received all the information or that faithfulness requires that their perspectives never change. He insists that on the journey, over time, the

Spirit would teach them new-to-them things that have always been true, they just couldn't bear them at that moment. What if we had access to a real-life, bona fide time machine? Can you imagine if we went back two thousand years—or even just two hundred years—and brought one of our ancestors into our present? How would they react to cars, airplanes, or iPhones? They would not be able to fathom such technological advances, and they'd probably accuse us of dabbling in some sort of dark arts. They wouldn't have any frame of reference for such things, but in some profound way, all these technological advances we enjoy, and all those still to come, can be traced back to our ancestors doing their creative best with the information they had available to them in their time. After all, we don't have cars without wheels, do we?

The Bible invites us into this creative reimagination of and renegotiation with what came before us. When we learn something new—say, that the solar system is not geocentric, not heliocentric—that is not a threat to our faith or to God; it's actually an invitation from the Spirit to expand our understanding and move into even more truth. In this way, the Bible isn't a collection of "timeless truths" as much as it's a kind of collective diary that shares with us the journey of those who came before us and an invitation to responsibly do our part in the ongoing search for truth and meaning. The Bible doesn't answer all the questions or tell us everything we ought to think. Instead, it shows us the trajectory of the Spirit, how the Spirit moved and led our spiritual ancestors back then, in order to help cultivate an awareness in us of where to look for the Spirit's movement in our own moment.

If any of this is true, why would anyone want to weaponize the Bible? There are a few key reasons—impulses even—that lie beneath a weaponized Scripture. First, we tend to use the Bible as a weapon when we have a fear-based view of God. While to my knowledge I have never physically thrown a Bible at someone, in the past I did regularly scour the Bible for verses to share with others (whether they asked or consented or not) in order to make them do what I thought God wanted them to do. If we think that God is most concerned about our correct theology, as if any of us has or even could have a 100 percent correct theology, then we might turn to the Bible for some motivational messages that would help those we care about escape the eternal torment that awaits them if they don't change their minds.

Several years ago, I took my oldest son to his first big-time professional wrestling event. He was newly interested, and I grew up a fan, so I knew we'd have a good time. When we lined up outside Bridgestone Arena in Nashville, I remember suddenly hearing a slightly muffled, but also amplified, voice rising above the sounds of the crowd. I turned to the right and saw a few guys, one of whom was standing on a milk crate and talking into a megaphone. The others held poorly made signs that reflected the message being shared. To sum it up, basically everyone who had any beliefs that diverged from the speaker and his friends would not being going to heaven. God was, in this view, a cosmic Santa Claus, just less generous. The list had been made and checked twice, and most everyone was in big trouble. My son had absolutely no frame of reference for what was happening. His only understanding of God was loving, expansive, and inclusive. I remember thinking two things in that moment: One, I am so glad my kid doesn't understand this. And two, I get it. When your vision of God is angry, exacting, and wrathful, preaching to strangers that they are all going to hell is the only option. I mean, how could we not?!? The stakes are eternally high. So it makes all the sense in the world, from that perspective, to do whatever it takes to save people from God's wrath.

Further, we use the Bible as a weapon when we prooftext passages without considering the context. As we saw above, this approach to the Bible ignores the diversity of Scripture on key issues, opting instead for focusing only on passages or texts that affirm a preconceived interpretation, usually one that intends to exclude a specific group or community. This is how I was taught to read the Bible—as a collection of truths and expectations for humanity, totally divorced from the people and contexts that produced these texts. The fact is that you and I can probably build a case for anything using the Bible, if we read it looking for prooftexts. There's an anxiety that underlies this approach that ties back to a fear-based view of God that tells us that God really wants to make sure we are right, that we have all the correct beliefs (if such were even possible). That anxiety sends us to the Bible looking for proof of our rightness and others' wrongness. What if God banks on the fact that we will have some things wrong? What if God understands the limits of our knowledge? What if God is more generous, compassionate, and patient than we could even begin to imagine or hope?

The best gig I have is that I get to be called "Dad" by five of the greatest humans that have ever existed. They are wonderful, each of them in their own unique ways. They also have limited knowledge based on their stage of life. How do you think I respond to them in those kinds of situations? I don't punish them, I teach them. Because their limited understanding is expected and part of their growth.

Friends, the good news is that the same is true for us. God understands all that we don't understand, and God isn't angry about it. After all, if we can be understanding and compassionate, can't God all the more? That's also why we have been gifted the Spirit—to help us learn and grow over time. There's probably a Bible verse to prove any point we'd want to make, and there's probably a book in any library that can do the same. Yet that's not how we engage a library, is it? We understand the diversity of experience and learning that is being shared. The same is true with the Bible. The Bible is a gift, not because it tells us the one thing we should think or believe, but because it inspires us to think and believe.

I wish—oh, how I wish—I could write these words from the lofty place of always getting this right. Alas, I write from the place of having been humiliated by the way I have previously engaged and used the Bible. Perhaps that is the real problem: *using* the Bible. The Bible is not intended to be used any more than our own family stories are intended to be used for some narrow, predetermined purpose. Not long ago I found myself on one of those ancestry sites that helps you figure out from where and from whom you came. The results of that exploration were interesting and unsettling. But that is the story of my family, the good, bad, and the ugly. That, friends, is what we have in the Bible. The story of the faith of our ancestors, including the way it grew, changed, and shifted over time. It's also the trajectory from which we are invited to launch our own contributions to that story.

My maternal grandfather was a fundamentalist Free Will Baptist pastor. He was a good man, and in the eleven years I had with him his passion for truth shaped me in ways that have led me to become who I am today. I also recognize that, if he were still here these thirty-two years later, he would disagree with me on all this vehemently. At the same time, it is what he instilled in me that led me to this place, this perspective, this moment.

Life is rarely linear. It winds and twists and does unexpected things. That is also the story of our sacred text. The Bible is a family history. Like the marks on the doorframe that show our growth, the Bible invites us to see how our ancestor grew over a thousand years or so. It does not limit further growth. It does not demand to be weaponized and used to coerce others to agree with us. Like a library or a family tree, it invites us to take it seriously, to learn from where we've been, and to step up and play our part faithfully today.

That is perhaps the most important point to make. The Bible is not just a collection of texts about the past. For sure, it is a collection of texts from the past that show us how those who came before us struggled, questioned, failed, celebrated, grew, and experienced their humanity. But it's not only that. It's also an invitation, one not to be weaponized and used to coerce others but to inspire us to play our part in this ever-unfolding story. There is so much good work in front of us, and the library that is the Bible continually calls us to step into that responsibility. We read it, learn from it, and are shaped by it precisely so that we can make our contribution to the story that has been, is, and will continue to be, long after our time is over. That practice, of understanding both the context of the Bible and how it interacts with our own, is an antidote to this misuse of Scripture.

We have explored how and why the Bible has been weaponized, and now we turn to specific instances in which the Bible has been used in this way. In the remaining pages of this book, we will see how the Bible has been used to defend and uphold patriarchy and misogyny, homophobia, racism, and nationalism. We'll also explore the alternative approaches and perspectives that value the well-being of all of God's children.

2

Gender Equality

SCHOOL IS IN SESSION

In the fall of 1999, I began my first semester as an undergraduate at Pikeville College (now called the University of Pikeville). That first semester was filled with the usual slate of classes all college freshmen take—basic English and math courses, along with history and psychology. The final course added to my load was an elective religion class, Introduction to the Hebrew Bible. I had signed on for this particular class with much trepidation. My religious upbringing, while I didn't know it or have the language for it at the time, was very conservative, bordering on fundamentalist. There was a healthy skepticism that had been drilled into me about the religion department at public colleges and universities. Even as I enrolled in the course I was cautioned, "This might ruin your faith if you aren't careful."

I, however, wasn't worried. I knew the Bible well and was well-versed in our doctrines and interpretations. There was a prooftext for just about everything, and I had spent hours upon hours memorizing them. If anything, I thought, I might change the professor's mind and they might even get saved. Ah, the unfounded confidence of an eighteen-year-old white male. Needless to say, things did not go as I'd planned.

On the first day of class, to my surprise, Dr. Grizzard entered the classroom. It was surprising because she was, well, a she. In my tradition, women were not empowered to lead—to teach, to preach, to have a shaping voice in discussions of interpretation. A woman could not give a sermon, though on certain days one might be permitted to share a testimony. Nor could women lead adult Bible studies. Their teaching was relegated to leading Sunday school classes for children and youth, an important role to be sure, but also a limited one.

In fact, it became abundantly clear and obvious growing up that women were only empowered to do the tasks and assume the roles in our church that the men preferred to avoid. No one balked at a woman planning, executing, and cleaning up after a potluck, for example. Outside of those kinds of jobs, however, women were rarely heard when it came to the serious business of the church. Their main job was to submit to the leadership and guidance of their father, husband, pastor—any male of authority.

When Dr. Grizzard walked in, I knew that I had my work cut out for me. It would be up to me to let her know that she was exercising unbiblical authority by teaching a classroom full of adult (if you could call us that) males. Thank God I didn't have the chance. In that first class, what is usually a throwaway day of introductions and syllabi, Dr. Grizzard began to speak about the Bible, its sources and origins, with such passion that I was left completely stunned speechless. I had been taught to fear this kind of talk and this kind of person. However, in that moment, the opposite was happening. I was enthralled. She was opening up the Bible for me in new ways, which also helped begin to make sense of some of the questions I'd been secretly harboring about certain biblical texts that just seemed to be at odds with each other. Further, the idea of her being unqualified to teach because of her gender seemed so...silly. What about her gender made all her effort, education, wisdom, and passion inappropriate? To say I was unsettled by the experience would be an understatement, but it was also invigorating. Her teaching made me love the Bible and engage with it more than ever. That couldn't be a bad thing, could it?

My unexpected experience and preconceived understanding had collided in that classroom, and I knew I had work to do. The understanding I had inherited was grounded in a specific way of reading and interpreting the Bible. That being the case, I knew that I needed to go back to the Bible, to seriously study and interrogate the texts that had been used to cement this view in my thinking, and to look for other texts that might shed more light on the subject. What I discovered was a series of familiar texts that, when placed within their ancient and biblical contexts, suddenly weren't so obvious or clear in their meanings. I also found other texts, those that my tradition had largely ignored, minimized, or explained away, that offered an alternative understanding of the role of women in the early Jesus communities. In the remainder of this chapter, we will examine these texts and counter-texts, exploring what we can know about their context and how they challenge the church of the twenty-first century to a more expansive, not more restrictive, understanding.

SILENCE AND SUBMISSION

The first text that was oft quoted to silence and subjugate women is found in the first pages of the Bible. The story of Adam and Eve eating the forbidden fruit, in my understanding back in my college days, meant that women being submissive to men was something that God intended to be woven into the very fabric of creation. It was God's plan all along, we thought. But why did we think that?

In the story of Genesis 3, the first people, at the instigation of a talking snake, disobey the command of God about the fruit of which trees were fair game for food. According to the Genesis 2 creation story, after God formed the first human out of the dirt (the word for "human" in Hebrew, *adam*, is connected to the word for ground, *adamah*) and then turns to cultivating an environment for this human.

> The LORD God planted a garden in Eden, in the east, and there he put the man whom he had formed. Out of the ground the LORD God made to grow every tree that is pleasant to the sight and good for food, the tree of life also in the midst of the garden, and the tree of the knowledge of good and evil.
>
> (Genesis 2:8b-9)

This was an Eden, a paradise, for this first human to live, work, and play in. There were boundaries, however. Not all trees were to be sources of nourishment for Adam. In fact, one specific tree would do the opposite, it would create death and not life.

> The LORD God took the man and put him in the garden of Eden to till it and keep it. And the LORD God commanded the man, "You may freely eat of every tree of the garden, but of the tree of the knowledge of good and evil you shall not eat, for in the day that you eat of it you shall die."
>
> (Genesis 2:15-17)

The debate has raged for millennia about the tree of the knowledge of good and evil and its forbidden fruit. What was it? An apple? A pear? Sex? Why was it even forbidden in the first place? While not the focus here, I feel compelled to offer a suggestion. What if the tree of the knowledge of good and evil represents exactly what it says? What if it is about deciding what, or who, is good and what, or who, is evil? Perhaps, then, the story is about what we have often done as a species after making judgments about who and what are good and acceptable—we take that judgment and use it as a pretext for violence. The fruit (deciding we are the judge) of that tree does often lead to the death God warned about, doesn't it?

The fallout that resulted from eating the fruit was swift and immense. God comes to these first people, calls them out of their hiding place, and shares with them the results of their actions. What God says to the woman in the story has become a significant prooftext to limit the role and equality of women for untold generations.

> *To the woman [God] said,*
> *"I will make your pangs in childbirth exceedingly great;*
>   *in pain you shall bring forth children,*
> *yet your desire shall be for your husband,*
>   *and he shall rule over you."*
>
> *(Genesis 3:16)*

"See," proponents of this perspective say, "God says here that women shall be ruled by men. It's God's will, and to do anything else would be unfaithful." The author of 1 Timothy would offer a hearty amen to that. While this particular text is attributed to Paul, the vast majority of scholars find both language and ideas present in 1 Timothy that date much later than the life of the historical Paul. Many suggest that 1 Timothy, along with the rest of the letters grouped and called the Pastoral

Epistles (2 Timothy and Titus), reflect not the fifties or sixties of the first century but sometime in the early second century instead. Additionally, we know it was common in the ancient world for writers to claim the identity of other well-known figures in order to enjoy the authority that person would have. The writings that follow this practice are called *pseudepigrapha*. I find it to be a compelling argument. With that in mind, this is how an unknown author, writing in Paul's name, interpreted Genesis 3:

> *Let a woman learn in silence with full submission. I do not permit a woman to teach or to have authority over a man; she is to keep silent. For Adam was formed first, then Eve, and Adam was not deceived, but the woman was deceived and became a transgressor. Yet she will be saved through childbearing, provided they continue in faith and love and holiness, with self-control.*
>
> *(1 Timothy 2:11-15)*

Both the order of their creation and their tasting of the forbidden fruit is all this author needed to assign the bulk of the blame on Eve as a representative of all women. That's why, according to this author, women must be silent and learn from men, because the women are so easily deceived. (Note that there's no mention here of the fact that Adam went along with it. Makes his judgment questionable, doesn't it?) Their best bet for salvation is to have babies and stay quiet, according to this writer.

The weaponization potential of this text in particular has become all too evident. At Donald Trump's second Inaugural Prayer Service in 2025, the Episcopal Bishop Mariann Budde gave a sermon in which she asked the newly (re)minted president for something that has become controversial these days: mercy. Specifically, she called his administration to do justice and extend compassion to those in communities he has previously attacked.

> In the name of our God, I ask you to have mercy upon the people in our country who are scared now. There are gay, lesbian and transgender children in Democratic, Republican and independent families. Some who fear for their lives. They may not be citizens or have the proper documentation, but the vast majority of immigrants are not criminals. They pay taxes and are good neighbors. They are faithful members of our churches and mosques, synagogues.

While this request, this call and challenge, situate Budde firmly in the biblical tradition of speaking truth to power, Bishop Budde was met with a swift and vitriolic response by supporters of the president. In their attempt to criticize the bishop for "bringing politics into the pulpit," they also quoted 1 Timothy 2:11-15 to prove that, in their interpretation, the bishop should not occupy her office or be giving sermons in the first place. In doing so, they ignored scores of texts that call us all to do the very thing the bishop asked of the president.

The weaponization of the Bible was happening in real time, right before our eyes.

To be sure, this is a perspective that shows up in other texts in the New Testament, but it should be noted that each of them reflects some similar perspectives to what we find in 1 Timothy. In both Ephesians and Colossians, in what is called the Household Codes because they offer instruction for family life, the idea of women submitting to male leadership is present. These are also texts that represent what we saw above about some letters attributed to Paul—letters scholars believe were written in Paul's name after his death in order to piggyback on his authority. In this case, these two letters are dated sometime between the eighties and nineties of the first century, or roughly twenty to thirty years after Paul lived. The two texts read similarly, meaning that one of the authors likely knew of the other text and borrowed from it.

> *Wives, be subject to your husbands, as is fitting in the Lord.*
> *(Colossians 3:18)*

> *Wives, be subject to your husbands as to the Lord, for the husband is the head of the wife just as Christ is the head of the church, his body, and is himself its Savior. Just as the church is subject to Christ, so also wives ought to be, in everything, to their husbands.*
> *(Ephesians 5:22-24)*

A similar command appears in another later text, 1 Peter (written around 110 CE), that echoes and expands the ideas found in Colossians and Ephesians. In this text, the author commands women to be submissive so that, if their husbands aren't part of their faith they might be won over by the obedience of their wives. The practical implications of these texts matter. Churches and pastors have used prooftexts like these to silence women in the church and home, but they have also been quoted to command women to stay in abusive relationships. The church should be at the forefront of condemning abuse and helping the abused, not excusing abuse and covering for the abuser.

There is one final text that deserves mention, and it, too, is questionable. Throughout all of the biblical books that are almost universally agreed to be authentic letters by Paul— 1 Thessalonians, Galatians, 1 Corinthians, 2 Corinthians, Philemon, Philippians, and Romans—there is a single section that offers a perspective similar to what we've already seen. That text is found in 1 Corinthians 14 in a discussion of gifts of the Spirit.

> *Women should be silent in the churches. For they are not permitted to speak but should be subordinate, as the law also says. If there is something they want to learn, let them ask their husbands at home. For it is shameful for a woman to speak in church.*
>
> (1 Corinthians 14:34-35)

Interestingly, this appears to be a later scribal addition. Remember, there was no printing press at the time, so any written works had to be copied by hand, and sometimes the scribes doing that labor inserted their own or someone else's words. And how have scholars come to that conclusion about 1 Corinthians 14? Because when it is removed from the text, the discussion Paul is having about prophecy makes perfect sense uninterrupted. It seems at some point in the transmission and copying of this text, the idea of women being silent in the church was added into 1 Corinthians 14 even though it blatantly contradicts what Paul says in other letters (which we will see shortly).

Even if we cast aside everything I have said up until this point about authorship, dates, and scribal additions, the idea that women are to be silent and submissive runs into another challenge. In other places, Paul argues precisely the opposite viewpoint.

TRANSGRESSING THE CULTURAL BOUNDARIES

The entirety of the Bible was written in a world immersed in patriarchy. Now, if you'd have asked anybody at that time, What does patriarchy mean? they would look at you like you had three heads. That's because, for them, it was just the world and order they knew. It was how the world worked, and that was assumed to be the product of divine intention, not human injustice. Yet within that world, another idea began to emerge.

In the Gospels, especially Luke, Jesus includes female disciples in ways that would have been shocking to observers. He even engaged women, like the woman at the well in John 4 or the Syrophoenician woman in Mark 7, in ways that would have transgressed cultural boundaries and raised eyebrows.

Perhaps our best window into how some of the early Jesus communities functioned in this regard is Paul's authentic letters, because they predate the earliest Gospel by ten to twenty years. Galatians is believed to be one of Paul's earliest letters, and within that text we find what is understood to be an early baptismal formula. Some call it a baptismal creed that reflects the radical understanding of early Jesus followers about their movement. It is a text that I can't remember hearing preached or even addressed in my upbringing, I assume because it would have presented a stark contrast and challenge to our dogma. For Paul, baptism and being "clothed in Christ" initiates a person into a new reality altogether.

> *As many of you as were baptized into Christ have clothed yourselves with Christ. There is no longer Jew or Greek; there is no longer slave or free; there is no longer male and female, for all of you are one in Christ Jesus. And if you belong to Christ, then you are Abraham's offspring, heirs according to the promise.*
> *(Galatians 3:27-29)*

In his fantastic book *Desire of the Everlasting Hills: The World Before and After Jesus*, Thomas Cahill argues that Paul's statement in Galatians represents a first in human history:

The cosmic Christ, whose glory knocked Paul from his horse on the road to Damascus, who sums up in himself the whole of the created universe, eventually leads Paul to thoughts that no one had ever had before—thoughts about the equality of all human beings before God. In this ancient world of masters and slaves, conquerors and conquered, a world that articulates at every turn, precisely and publicly, who's on top, who's on bottom, Paul writes the unthinkable…."In Christ Jesus"—in the ultimate cosmic reality—there can be no power relationships. The primitive Church was the world's first egalitarian society.[1]

This statement might be slightly exaggerated. It probably wasn't Paul's original idea, nor was it shared by everyone who found Jesus compelling. But it does represent a layer of the early Jesus movement that lived and practiced in ways that were dramatically different from and challenging to the ways the dominant cultures, specifically the culture of imperial Rome, carved up the world. Every relationship in that world was about power and hierarchy. For Paul, the cross of Jesus is where those values died. For him, dying and being buried with Christ in baptism also meant being raised into a new life, complete with new values that challenged and contradicted those of the dominant culture.

The hierarchies that were so deep, prevalent, and controlling in his world were now irrelevant and obsolete in light of Jesus and the kingdom of God vision. Specifically,

Paul says that the way the world had been divided up between insiders and outsiders, powerful men and subservient women, and rich and poor were not categories that held meaning in the Jesus community. The presence, the here and now accessibility of God's kingdom meant that Jesus's followers must begin to live differently, even as the dominant culture operated under the stratification of business as usual.

The tension of this way of living the Kingdom life in the system of empire shows up in other places, like 1 Corinthians 11. There, Paul is frustrated by the way the Corinthians have turned the Lord's Supper, an egalitarian feast in which all members shared the same food and drink, into another opportunity for the wealthy to shame and distinguish themselves from those who were poor and enslaved. This, according to Paul, was an abuse that transformed their not-so-shared-meal into anything but the Lord's Supper. He goes so far as to say that when they gather for the meal and eat it in ways that emphasize hierarchy, they are doing more harm than good. He calls them to remember the way Jesus ate meals and challenges them to practice the same kind of generosity and radical inclusivity. For Paul, inequality among members, whether around socioeconomic status or gender, was a sign that the empire was transforming the church and not the other way around.

Further evidence that the historical Paul embraced women as equals, specifically in church leadership, is found in what is likely the final letter we have from Paul, the Letter to the

Romans. The longest of Paul's correspondence known to us, it ends with what is likely a personal recommendation for the courier who brought the text to Rome, a woman named Phoebe.

> I commend to you our sister Phoebe, a deacon of the church at Cenchreae, so that you may welcome her in the Lord, as is fitting for the saints, and help her in whatever she may require from you, for she has been a benefactor of many and of myself as well.
> (Romans 16:1-2)

Notice first that she is likely the one entrusted to carry this letter to Rome, which was no small responsibility. She would also, as the bearer of Paul's words, offer the reading of them to the church and assist in the interpretation and explication of what Paul wrote. She was being entrusted as Paul's representative to speak on his behalf. She is also referred to as a deacon, which carries the connotation of leadership, and she is a supporter of Paul's work. And she's just the tip of the iceberg.

In Romans 16 Paul mentions twenty-nine people, twenty-seven of whom are named. Of those twenty-nine, one-third of them are women, most of who are assigned some kind of leadership responsibility. There's Prisca (sometimes also called Priscilla), who, along with her husband Aquila, "risked their necks" (v. 4) for Paul. There's also a Mary, "who has worked very hard for you" (v. 6), and Junia, who is called "prominent among the apostles" (v. 7). Some translators have tried to render Junia as Junias, using the male form of the name, because they could not fathom Paul celebrating a woman in that capacity. We also hear about Tryphaena, Tryphosa, and Persis, all women who worked hard for the movement. There are others still, including Rufus's mother, who was like a mother to Paul.

If we have such evidence of female leadership in the early Jesus movement, why do some Christians and churches refuse to affirm their call and gifting in leadership? Why does part of the New Testament do so, while other parts say the opposite?

Let me address the latter question first. How do we go from overturning hierarchy in the authentic letters of Paul to the enforcing of it in the later texts written in his name? We could just chalk it up to differences in perspective. The writers of those later letters disagreed with Paul and decided to use his authority to make their perspective normative in the church. Perhaps that is part of it. I think, however, that there might be another reason. Can you imagine, as the Jesus movement spread into the wider, patriarchal Roman world, how their gatherings might have been perceived? How might Roman women who were not invited to enjoy meals with the men around them, but only serve them, feel when women in the Jesus community were sitting at the table as equals? Can you envision a scenario in which these early communities were being pressured by the wider culture, perhaps even the state, to stop upsetting the order that stabilized the power structures of their society? Perhaps, it is at least possible, the Pastorals are responding to that pressure.

Now let's return to the first question I posed. Why does the New Testament say different, even conflicting things about the role of women? Might I suggest it's because of what we learned in the previous chapter? The Bible is not a book, but a collection of texts that reflect different times, places, and pressures. To put it another way, the Bible is not mono-vocal, meaning it does not speak with one voice. It is multivocal; it speaks in many voices. Our task is to study and wrestle with the voices we find there and as a community of Jesus followers, try to discern what the Spirit is calling us to in this moment. That can be a scary task, I understand. It is often easier to just be told what to think and do. But that is not the process to which God has invited us. God is looking for our participating in creating the future.

I can't help but think that one of the reasons some branches of Christianity resist a more expansive and inclusive understanding is because they are being led by men who are more concerned, whether consciously or subconsciously (I'll leave that to them and God), with protecting their power than reflecting the beauty, complexity, and diversity of a God who made people in God's image. That refusal has robbed large swaths of the church of a significant reflection of God's image and cut us off from a perspective that we desperately need to have in our decisions and interpretations. As a result, the church has found itself complicit in abuse and covering up for abusers, it sometimes has a hypermasculine focus that distorts our faith communities and shows an absence of much-needed voices. My sincere hope is that my Christian siblings who resist gender equality in the church (and the world for that matter) will have an encounter like I did with Dr. Grizzard that opens and expands their hearts and minds. That's why I have dedicated this book to her memory. She lived out her calling with great skill, and it changed my life. I am truly grateful.

3

LGBTQ+ Inclusion

A HOLY MOMENT

Several years ago, a close friend reached out to me and asked if we could go to lunch. A few days later we sat together at a small table at a local restaurant and caught up on the latest news from our lives. It was enjoyable and needed, but I didn't understand why he had been a little cryptic in his request to get together. After we finished lunch, we rode back to my office, and that's when his mood turned serious. He was clearly nervous, fidgeting a little, avoiding eye contact.

"I need to tell you something," he said, "and when I do it's going to change everything. It will end our friendship."

What could it be, I wondered. What could possibly end our friendship if I knew about it? Was he some sort of serial killer? Had he participated in a series of bank robberies and was now going to be on the lam for the foreseeable future?

"I can't imagine that will be the case," I said, trying to reassure him.

"Oh, it will be," he said, taking a deep breath. "Because I'm gay."

In that moment it seemed like a ton of bricks was taken off of him, only to be replaced with two tons. He had spoken out loud, for the first time, a secret that he'd held as long as he could remember. The freedom of speaking that truth was met with the expected consequence of immediate condemnation and rejection.

As tears welled up in his eyes I stood up, opened my arms, and gave him the biggest hug I could offer. "I love you," I told him. "This doesn't change that; it actually deepens it. I am so honored that you trusted me with this, and I want you to know that I support you, and I celebrate the fullness of who God made you to be."

I have been honored to be in a similar place with many friends over the years. When someone trusts you deeply enough to come out to you, to share that important part of who they are, it is such a gift—a holy moment. What struck me as I embraced my friend in that significant moment was that he already knew my position on LGBTQ+ inclusion. We had talked many times about my journey toward becoming an affirming Christian, about the fact that I wanted to be a good ally to that beloved community of people. How could he think this news would change my love and care for him?

The more I thought about it, the more the reason became clear. The church has, for so long, been a source of condemnation, shame, rejection, and exclusion for members of the LGBTQ+ community. So many have been told that they must choose between who God made them to be and belonging in the family of God. For too long churches have hidden behind disingenuous phrases like "All are welcome," when in reality there is a massive asterisk attached. The fine print reveals that LGBTQ+ people are welcome to attend and give their money to the church, but beyond that they are excluded from the full life of the community. Their love is considered unholy, their babies can't be dedicated, baptized, or confirmed, and they aren't empowered to use their gifts of leadership and service. The truth is a conditional, partial welcome is no welcome at all. When a church hides behind such a false pretense, people are always going to be the collateral damage of maintaining the status quo. That is why over the years I have worked to be very clear about what I mean around this topic. I believe our LGBTQ+ siblings are exactly who God created them to be and should be fully included in the life of the church without qualification or footnote.

Before we go further in a discussion about the full and un-asterisked inclusion of the LGBTQ+ community in the church, let me offer one final thought. This is not an issue to be debated. These are humans, people, image bearers of God, and they deserve to be loved and valued for who they are, not in spite of it. Not as a favor or act of compassion, but as their birthright as God's children. In all of our conversations, both in this book and in your own discussions about it, let's not lose sight of the very real human beings at the core of this conversation.

HOW DID I END UP HERE?

You might be wondering how I ended up holding this position, so let me offer a little biographical data. I was not raised in a liberal, progressive, or affirming denomination. My earliest church experience was in what can only be described as a form of Christian fundamentalism. In the Free Will Baptist church of my youth, we were King James only, women couldn't speak or wear pants, and we made hellfire and damnation regular topics of conversation. Later, we made what was perceived as a liberal move by becoming Southern Baptists. Again, while more liberal than my Free Will experience, we still held similar positions. Reading the NIV instead, we still limited the role of women to essentially party planning and daycare services. In both traditions, we knew without a doubt that being LGBTQ+ was a sin, perhaps the gravest sin one could commit. I held that perspective for the first two decades of my life, and then everything changed.

When I am asked how I became LGBTQ+ affirming, I immediately warn people that this story is not spectacular. I didn't have a vision, hear a voice, or anything like that. It was a realization that came to me as I was sitting with dear friends who, like the one at the beginning of this chapter, trusted me enough to bare their souls to me. In those holy moments I realized that nothing in me wanted to condemn my friends. I knew them, after all. I knew their lives, how deeply they loved God, how seriously they took their faith. The fruit of the Spirit was abundant in them, so how, if Jesus was right about knowing people by their fruit, could I look at these friends of mine and say that they were sinning or leaving the faithful path? They simply wanted to be their full, authentic selves, not to abandon their faith.

I found myself wanting for these friends all that I had wanted and hoped for myself—love, happiness, meaningful connection. But then I had a problem. My heart was there, but my head was playing catch-up. *What do I do*, I wondered, *with the Bible?* This tension between head and heart led me to go back to the Bible, to engage the so-called "clobber passages," a series of texts that have been cherry-picked and assumed to condemn and exclude the LGBTQ+ community. What I learned was fascinating and only deepened my commitment to being an affirming ally.

CLOBBERING THE CLOBBER PASSAGES

When I went back to examine the seven passages that collectively make up the "clobber passages," I was surprised by what I learned. These texts are found in both Old and New

Testaments, and each deserves an extensive explanation that lies outside the bounds of this book. In the time we have, I will introduce the texts, briefly offer some of what I discovered in my research, and at the end of the chapter I will share a few recommended resources that go much deeper into each of these passages.

The first text comes from Genesis 19 and is the well-known story of the destruction of Sodom and Gomorrah. This text is often assumed to be about God destroying these ancient cities because they were wicked, specifically because the inhabitants were engaging in same-sex relationships. I treat this story in depth in my book *Context: Putting Scripture in Its Place*, but I will share a brief summary of why this reading is not only insufficient but also just contextually unfounded.

First, the issue in the story of Sodom isn't about mutually consensual sex between people of the same sex. It's a story about attempted sexual assault. Those are wildly different things. This story is drawing on the central and vital ancient understanding of hospitality. In the ancient world that gave us this story, the refusal to practice generous hospitality was a grave failure. There are similar stories, like the account of Baucis and Philemon, that mirror the details of the Sodom story, and those stories are explicitly about the refusal of hospitality to strangers. Other voices in Scripture confirm this reading.

Notice how the prophet Ezekiel addresses the sin of Sodom:

> *This was the guilt of your sister Sodom: she and her daughters had pride, excess of food, and prosperous ease but did not aid the poor and needy. They were haughty and did abominable things before me; therefore I removed them when I saw it.*
>
> *(Ezekiel 16:49-50)*

We'll address the idea of "abomination" shortly, but for now the point to notice is that the problem in Sodom was having abundance and being indifferent to the needs of the poor. The Gospels also offer Jesus's perspective on this story, and you might be surprised how he addressed it. While preparing his disciples to be sent out to announce the kingdom of God as a present and accessible reality, Jesus gives his followers these instructions:

> *As you enter the house, greet it. If the house is worthy, let your peace come upon it, but if it is not worthy, let your peace return to you. If anyone will not welcome you or listen to your words, shake off the dust from your feet as you leave that house or town. Truly I tell you, it will be more tolerable for the land of Sodom and Gomorrah on the day of judgment than for that town.*
>
> *(Matthew 10:12-15)*

For Jesus the story of Sodom was a story of a people who refused to extend welcome and hospitality. Next we turn to two passages found in the Book of Leviticus. These texts are part what is known as the *Holiness Code*, a series of laws and commands that call for Israel to be separate and distinct from surrounding cultures. These texts are similar, with a slight, but significant, difference between them.

> *You shall not lie with a male as with a woman; it is an abomination.*
>
> *(Leviticus 18:22)*

> *If a man lies with a male as with a woman, both of them have committed an abomination; they shall be put to death; their bloodguilt is upon them.*
>
> *(Leviticus 20:13)*

These two texts agree on the idea that for a male to have sex with a male like a man would with a woman, that it is an abomination. Leviticus 20, however, takes it to the extreme. Anyone caught doing such a thing should be killed, and it would be their own fault, the text says. While it might seem like a cut-and-dried text, I would caution against a rush to judgment. For example, these passages only focus on same-sex acts between males. Women are conspicuously absent here. They are not absent in other prohibitions in the Holiness Code, so this is not just reflecting the values of a patriarchal society. Women show up in many places in these chapters, just not in this prohibition. I do think patriarchy is at the core of these texts, however. The issue is not people of the same sex experiencing intimacy together.

The issue, in particular, is with a male being in the passive role of the relationship, thus being treated or in the position of a woman. For men in a patriarchal society, being treated as or placed in a similar role as a woman was considered to be a humiliation and something beneath a man. Women were disempowered, essentially treated as property. For a male to be in that role would be the ultimate societal embarrassment. If that shouldn't cause us to reconsider our patriarchal ideas and systems, I don't know what should. Seems to be a litmus test for the idea that we should treat others the way we want to be treated. This is not just an issue with these texts, but with human society as a whole. While most of our Jewish siblings have largely moved forward on both gender equality and LGBTQ+ inclusion, significant portions of the Christian tradition have, sadly, not. The two are deeply intertwined. It is hard to move toward inclusion of LGBTQ+ people when you still view women as less than men.

If you read the entire Holiness Code (Leviticus 17–26), you'll find that much of the issue is about keeping things separate and maintaining Israel's distinctness from the nations that surrounded them. Something was an abomination when it was considered *unclean*, i.e., something the nations might engage in or practice. At one point these identity markers were crucial for the people of Israel to maintain their culture and identity in the revolving door of empires that tried to erase them. When they called something abominable, it didn't mean sinful, it meant "something those other nations do." It was not a universal moral code but a specific religious and culture marker. Our lack of contextual understanding has distorted and weaponized this idea in disastrous ways. To put it succinctly: If we are not bothered by all the things most of us do that are also called abominations in Leviticus, why are these two texts still considered normative and binding for our understanding of human sexuality?

Next, we turn to four texts within the New Testament. Two of them are from the pen of the historical Paul, while two are not. Let's begin with Romans 1, an authentic text from Paul.

> *For this reason God gave them over to dishonorable passions. Their females exchanged natural intercourse for unnatural, and in the same way also the males, giving up natural intercourse with females, were consumed with their passionate desires for one another. Males committed shameless acts with males and received in their own persons the due penalty for their error.*
>
> *(Romans 1:26-27)*

In this introduction, Paul is writing about idolatry, and he is writing to a community that is dealing with a specific issue. Scholars date Romans to sometime in the 60s CE. Much had been happening in Rome that had impacted a community like the Roman church. We can surmise that before the year 49 CE the church in Rome was likely a community made up of both Jewish and Gentile followers of Jesus. No doubt they were navigating tensions and differences but finding a way to flourish together as Jesus followers. In the year 49 CE, however, the Roman emperor Claudius issued a decree that expelled the

Jewish population from Rome, which would have included those Jews who were part of the church there. This event is described by the Roman historian Suetonius and is also mentioned in chapter 18 of the Book of Acts. Eventually, after Claudius died in 54 CE, the decree was rescinded, and members of the Jewish community were permitted to reenter the city once again.

With that history in mind, consider how this might have played out in the church in Rome. What was a more diverse community comprised of Jews and Gentiles living together suddenly became completely Gentile. Then, several years later, the Jewish community returns, including some who were followers of Jesus and looking to participate again in that church community. Would there be difficulty reintegrating the two different communities into one? That seems to be part of the point of Paul's letter to the church in Rome, to encourage and call these two groups to put aside their differences and become one family.

That's why Paul begins the way he does. In chapter 1 he spends his time essentially pointing out why the Gentiles are problematic for the Jewish community—they engage in practices that are off-limits to Jews and practice the worship of idols. Paul isn't running down the Gentiles without a plan, however. He engages in what would be the common Jewish prejudice against Gentiles of the day in order to invite them to see things differently. At the start of chapter 2 he turns the argument around, onto his Jewish siblings and says, "Not so fast!" Notice the transition between describing the Gentiles and his appeal to his Jewish siblings:

> And since they [Gentiles] did not see fit to acknowledge God, God gave them over to an unfit mind and to do things that should not be done. They were filled with every kind of injustice, evil, covetousness, malice. Full of envy, murder, strife, deceit, craftiness, they are gossips, slanderers, God-haters, insolent, haughty, boastful, inventors of evil, rebellious toward parents, foolish, faithless, heartless, ruthless. They know God's decree, that those who practice such things deserve to die, yet they not only do them but even applaud others who practice them.

> Therefore you are without excuse, whoever you are, when you judge others, for in passing judgment on another you condemn yourself, because you, the judge, are doing the very same things.
>
> (Romans 1:28–2:1)

Paul is engaging in some hyperbole and other rhetorical turns here, attempting to show that Jews and Gentiles, whatever their cultural differences, are in the same boat, all in need of the grace of God. Romans 1 is part of a strategic argument, not a once-and-for-all declaration about same-sex relationships or LGBTQ+ inclusion in the church. I really believe that if Paul knew how his words would have been misinterpreted, taken out of context, and used to harm others, he'd probably have opted for a different example.

One final point should be made. In Romans 1, Paul says that "their females exchanged natural intercourse for unnatural, and in the same way also the males, giving up natural intercourse with females." This has led some interpreters to assume that Paul is calling LGBTQ+ people unnatural, but that is not the case. In Paul's day many kinds of sexual acts were considered "unnatural," which meant, among other things, any kind of sex that was not procreative. It means something more like "out of the ordinary," not "forbidden" or "immoral." On the contrary, in Romans 11:24 Paul describes God acting "contrary to nature" by grafting the wild olive tree, symbolizing Gentiles, into the cultivated olive tree, representing Jews. Surely Paul us not calling God's action of bringing these two groups together into one community immoral or sinful, right? This image would also be Paul's way of challenging Gentile prejudice against Jewish members of the community. For Paul, Gentiles are included, but Jews got there first. What we have in Romans is a pastor desperately trying to hold together a community, not a systematic theologian pontificating about the right doctrines.

The other text from Paul comes from 1 Corinthians 6:9-10 and is part of what is known as a "vice list." He is explaining to the Corinthian community the kind of behaviors that prevent God's kingdom from becoming a present, experiential reality.

> *Do you not know that wrongdoers will not inherit the kingdom of God? Do not be deceived! The sexually immoral, idolaters, adulterers, male prostitutes, men who engage in illicit sex, thieves, the greedy, drunkards, revilers, swindlers—none of these will inherit the kingdom of God.*
>
> *(1 Corinthians 6:9-10)*

In this passage the two phrases that are of interest are "male prostitutes" and "men who engage in illicit sex." This translation is a major upgrade from those that came before, especially the Revised Standard Version (RSV). When the New Testament of the RSV was published in 1946, these two phrases, represented by two different words in Greek, were collapsed into the word *homosexual*. It was the first time the word appeared in any translation of the Bible, and the repercussions of this (mis) translation have been immense. Thankfully, the New Revised Standard Version, Updated Edition has corrected the error.

The two words being translated in this passage are *malakoi* and *arsenokoitai*. *Malakoi* literally just means "soft." It could be used to refer to clothing, like in Matthew 11:8 as Jesus is talking about John the Baptizer, "What, then, did you go out to see? Someone dressed in soft robes? Look, those who wear soft robes are in royal palaces." But it was also used as a put-down against men that also belittled women in the process. To be *malakoi* could mean to be "too feminine." Again, we see the ancient understanding that to be compared to a woman is the worst possible thing, even though it is through the courage and strength of women we all arrive on the planet. However, the word also carries the connotation of being "undisciplined," or "unrestrained." What this shows us is that words in the ancient world, like our own, could carry many meanings. Context is key when engaging these texts.

The second word, *arsenokoitai* is a bit more tricky, because the meaning is unclear. It's a compound word that brings together the word for "male" (*arsen*) and the word for "bed" (*koite*), which can refer to the furniture on which we sleep but can also be used as a euphemism for sex. The other occurrence of this word comes in a text attributed, but not likely written, by Paul. In 1 Timothy 1, there is a similar vice list:

> Now we know that the law is good, if one uses it legitimately; this means understanding that the law is laid down not for the righteous but for the lawless and disobedient, for the godless and sinful, for the unholy and profane, for those who kill their father or mother, for murderers, the sexually immoral, men who engage in illicit sex, slave traders, liars, perjurers, and whatever else is contrary to the sound teaching that conforms to the glorious gospel of the blessed God, with which I was entrusted.
>
> (1 Timothy 1:8-11)

In the text above, "the sexually immoral" (*pornos*) refers to prostitution. The second phase, "men who engage in illicit sex" is, again, *arsenokoitai*. It's interesting that in both of these lists *arsenokoitai* occurs right before other dishonest and exploitative practices. It's also important to note that Paul nor "Paul" are describing who won't go to heaven, but more accurately, those who are keeping heaven from coming to earth. It is most likely that *arsenokoitai* refers to a practice like pederasty, an exploit-ative relationship between an adult male and a boy, which was common in the Roman world. This isn't a condemnation of a loving, consenting same-sex relationship. Instead, it is a condemnation of abuse and exploitation.

Finally, we come to the last text, found in Jude, and it will take little of our time. In this short letter, only twenty-five verses in total, dated sometime after the year 100 CE, the author is condemning those who have any understanding of faith in Jesus that diverges from his own. In that process, he writes, referring back to a text we've already examined:

> Likewise, Sodom and Gomorrah and the surrounding cities, which, in the same manner as they, indulged in sexual immorality and pursued unnatural lust, serve as an example by undergoing a punishment of eternal fire.
>
> (Jude 7:7)

As we've seen, the story of Sodom does not refer to same-sex relationships or sex acts, but to abuse and sexual assault. Jude is not deviating from that understanding. If you recall the story of Sodom, the beings that the people of Sodom tried to rape and abuse were angels, not humans. Jude's reference to "unnatural lust" here simply refers to that scenario. There's no there in terms of dealing with human sexuality.

These are the texts commonly referred to as "clobber passages," because they clobber the LGBTQ+ community. However, on their own, the truth is, they don't. They are texts that reflect ancient understandings and contexts, not ours. The contemporary relevance such passages have for us is to call us away from abuse, exploitation, and violence, and toward love, compassion, and justice.

One final note before we close this chapter. Today we talk about things like "sexual orientation" and "gender identity," because we have come to understand that these are valid and meaningful parts of human identity and expression. The world that produced the Bible had no such categories. To be sure, LGBTQ+ people existed then, just as they do now. The difference is that back then there was no understanding of these issues, just like there was no understanding that the sun was the center of the solar system or that germs cause our sickness. We learn these things over time as we make new discoveries, as the Spirit leads us into more truth as we can bear it. Surely it is time to repent of our treatment and expulsion of our queer siblings. We are not being magnanimous or benevolent by doing so. We are not doing something grand or good. We are ceasing doing something wrong and harmful. It is not our job to make space for them. It is our job to get out of the way so they can occupy the space that God has already made for them and to which God has called them.

4

White Christian Nationalism

A DARK DAY IN AMERICA

On January 6, 2021, I sat on my couch with my family to watch what is, in most instances, a pretty innocuous process every four years: the counting of electoral votes and the certification by Congress of the results of the recent presidential election. What would unfold that day, to our horror, was an insurrection, instigated by Donald Trump, the sitting president of the United States, in a desperate attempt to override the will of voters and to overthrow a free and fair election. What became clear very quickly is that this was not *just* a matter of politics.

On the lawn of the United States Capitol, gallows were constructed next to signs that read "Hang Mike Pence," the soon-to-be-former Vice President who was overseeing the peaceful transfer of power in the joint session that day. Among those signs and symbols were others, and they spoke volumes about what the insurrectionists thought about their action. There was a large banner that read "Jesus Saves," crosses, and rioters holding Bibles. This was a political event, to be sure, but it was also a religious one. Many of those who stormed the Capitol that day, broke into the building, and assaulted Capitol police offers were motivated by their religion—their Christian religion. This was further expressed in a prayer given by Jacob Chansley, also known as the "QAnon Shaman," at the dais in the Senate chamber. After the mob had taken control of the room, Chansley prayed:

> Let's all say a prayer in this sacred space. Thank you, Heavenly Father, for this opportunity to stand up for God-given unalienable rights. Thank you, Heavenly Father, for being the inspiration needed to these police officers to allow us into the building, to allow us to exercise our rights, to allow us to send a message to all the tyrants, the communists and the globalists that this is our nation, not theirs."[1]

It became abundantly clear that religion, specifically a belief that God and Jesus were supporting their actions, emboldened this group to act. They were taking back America for God. At the Capitol on January 6, 2021, white Christian nationalism was on full display for the whole world to see. All three of those words have particular meanings in this phrase, and in this chapter, we will explore how they functioned together to light the tinderbox that exploded on January 6, 2021. How did we get here? What happened that sent ordinary people into such a disinformation frenzy that they attempted to stop democracy in its tracks?

Watching those events transpire, and all that has happened in the years since, I was reminded that we didn't arrive at this point overnight. This has been a slow burn, a subtle but growing process. Memories came flooding back as I began to reflect. I was suddenly taken back in time, back to when I was a teenager and attending a local Baptist church. The stage in our church was framed by two flags, the American flag and the Christian flag. I recalled vivid memories of church services around Memorial Day, July Fourth, and Veterans Day that left me scratching my head, even as a sixteen-year-old. Why are we singing songs about and to America during the time we are also worshipping God? Why are we focused on how much greater and blessed and chosen our country is, in a gathering meant to remember the God who loves the whole world? It didn't fully compute, and it just felt off.

Then 9/11 happened, and suddenly being Christian also meant supporting preemptive wars and vilifying Muslims. It really seemed as if Christianity was at war with Islam, represented respectively by America and the countries in the Middle East with which we were in conflict. To even question America's wars in some church settings would lead to charges of heresy and unfaithfulness. It was during this time that a leader I really trusted told me, "You know, in the Old Testament God commanded Israel to kill the Canaanites. God might be calling us to do something similar with Muslims." I could not believe what I was hearing. There is no way, I thought, that this is what God is like or what God wants.

It was a chilling moment, and one that, looking back, jump-started my process of waking up to some unfortunate truths about both my faith and my country. After all, aren't Christians and Americans always the "good guys"? Aren't we always on the side of truth and justice? Doesn't being a good Christian also mean being a good American? Hasn't America been chosen by God, like Israel in the Bible, to be God's representative nation and implement God's will on earth?

Before we continue, let me offer this disclaimer. First, I am grateful to be a Christian. I love my faith. I love the Bible. Most of all, I love Jesus. His message is, I believe, a transformative announcement of good news. That is why it grieves me so deeply when some of our Christian siblings behave in ways that are counter to Jesus's teaching, all the while claiming his support for their actions.

Second, I am grateful to be an American. Our country has problems, as all countries do. But I am glad to be part of this republic, and I feel fortunate to have been born and spent my life in it. At the same time, I also do not believe that America is better, more important, or more favored by God than anyone else. We are all God's beloved children, aren't we? The same is true for other religions. I am a committed Christian and will be for life. It is my "mother tongue," so to speak. I can learn to converse in other languages, but when I stub my toe I'm screaming in English. If I seem cynical at times about either my faith or my country, know that underneath it all there is a hope and resilience that keeps me going. I don't think we've seen the best days for either yet, if we choose to keep going toward love, peace, and justice. We can't make America or Christianity great again, but we can help to make them better in certain ways for the first time. Neither has fully reached their possibility or potential for liberation, freedom, and human flourishing. Not yet.

My wife and I have five amazing kids. On a regular basis they will tell us that we are the best mom and dad in the whole world. Can you imagine if I universalized that? If I took that literally? If I insisted to everyone that it was I, and not anyone else, who occupied the role of "Best Dad Ever"? Wouldn't that miss the point? That is the language of devotion. It's poetry. And I am grateful that they believe that is true, but it was never a competition to begin with, was it? That is how I hold my faith and my country, with gratitude and also knowing that people of other faiths and countries might feel the same about theirs.

WHAT DO WE MEAN BY WHITE CHRISTIAN NATIONALISM?

Before we discuss white Christian nationalism and why it's so problematic, it is important to define our terms so that we ensure we are all talking about the same thing. There are several possible definitions, all with the same general shape and scope. The particular definition I am using in this chapter comes from Jemar Tisby, a historian and the author of the *New York Times* bestseller *The Color of Compromise*. In an Instagram post he shared what I think is an accessible, concise, but informative definition. Tisby defines white Christian nationalism as "an ethnocultural ideology that uses Christian symbolism to create a permission structure for the acquisition of political power and social control." The last part is, I think, key. The point is gaining power and control in order to force others into the specific worldview, values, and beliefs of this particular group. Let's explore each of these in more detail and depth.

WHITE: AN ETHNOCULTURAL IDEOLOGY

In the next chapter we will explore racism specifically, but it needs to be addressed briefly here as well. The reality is white Christian nationalism is an ideology—a way of seeing, interpreting, and ordering the world—that holds up European and Western civilization as the best, superior to all other cultures and societies. This viewpoint is as American as apple pie. Europeans came to North America and, because they believed they were superior, displaced Indigenous peoples from their land, committing genocide in the process. Once dominance was established in the New World (it was really just new to them), then came the Atlantic slave trade, a practice supported by both the belief that white people were superior and that Christianity was supreme, over all other peoples and religions. In fact, they thought, by enslaving Africans and indoctrinating Indigenous peoples, these Christians were doing a service, something good and beneficial. In my own recent lifetime, I have heard people offer this as an excuse to defend America's racist past and present.

This process continued through emancipation and then segregation, upheld and codified by "separate but equal" Jim Crow laws that amounted to no equality at all. It is so important for us to remember that at the core of this cancer called white Christian nationalism, there is a direct line to the sins and evils of our past, and this ideology is intended to keep them in force in the present and future.

CHRISTIAN: GROUNDED IN DISTORTED SYMBOLS

White Christian nationalism makes use of the language and symbols of the Christian tradition, but it interprets them in ways that distort and transform them. As we've already seen, on January 6, 2021, there was no shortage of religious symbols or language. The name of Jesus was invoked, Bibles were clutched like magical talismans, and prayers were offered. January 6 and the movement that energized and enacted the insurrection were inspired by the faith of the participants.

The reality we must face is that Christian nationalism is not a new idea. It is not an invention of the twenty-first or even twentieth century. It dates back to a time when Christian leaders baptized the worst impulses and ideas in the name of expanding empires and increasing wealth. Let me offer an example of this from our history, the effects of which reverberate in our own time. In the fifteenth century, a series of edicts—called papal bulls—were issued by popes that served to justify and legitimate the Christian colonial project. One pope in particular issued a decree that is so reprehensible it would almost be unbelievable if it weren't still available to us.

In 1452, some forty years before Columbus sailed the ocean blue, Pope Nicholas V put forth a bull known as *Dum Diversas* that gave Christian explorers not only an excuse but divine permission to carry out every kind of dehumanizing act against non-Christian peoples in the lands they "discovered." Here's a short section to give you a feel for the kind of language and ideas that these papal decrees contained. In this document, the Pope authorized King Afonso V of Portugal to conquer those he called "Saracens [Muslims] and pagans."

Justly desiring that whatsoever concerns the integrity and spread of the faith, for which Christ our God shed his blood, shall flourish in the virtuous souls of the faithful…we grant to you by these present documents, with our Apostolic Authority, full and free permission to invade, search out, capture and subjugate the Saracens and pagans and any other unbelievers and enemies of Christ wherever they may be, as well as their kingdoms, duchies, counties, principalities, and other property…and to reduce their persons into perpetual slavery, and to apply and appropriate and convert to the use and profit of yourself and your successors, the Kings of Portugal, in perpetuity.[2]

It's shocking, isn't it? And it wasn't taken metaphorically. The permission in this decree unleashed hell everywhere explorers went, seizing land and people in the name of Jesus. This way of thinking was reinforced in later bulls by other popes and was even invoked as a legal doctrine—the doctrine of discovery—as recently as 2005 in a US Supreme Court decision that denied Indigenous peoples the right to regain full tribal control of territories that were stolen in the colonial project.

Of course, there are prooftexts that are cited to justify this merciless understanding as one Jesus would favor. The image of Jesus in the Book of Revelation paints Jesus to be more like Caesar, violent and brutal, than the Jesus of history and the Gospels. He slays his enemies and takes what he wants. That is a compelling vision for white Christian nationalists, and it serves as a permission structure for them. When your God is violent, and you are called to be like God, you can end up justifying all sorts of evil, just like the leader I mentioned earlier. If God called Israel to eradicate the Canaanites, why couldn't God call Christians to do the same to Muslims today? Why should we care about the suffering of Palestinians, Indigenous peoples, or immigrants when God has picked us to the exclusion of all other thems? It is the slipperiest of slopes.

I would be remiss if I didn't also mention the Great Commission, found in Matthew 28:18-20. In this passage, the risen Christ meets with and sends out his disciples to continue his work in the world.

> And Jesus came and said to them, "All authority in heaven and on earth has been given to me. Go therefore and make disciples of all nations, baptizing them in the name of the Father and of the Son and of the Holy Spirit and teaching them to obey everything that I have commanded you. And remember, I am with you always, to the end of the age."

"See," white Christian nationalists say, "we have a divine mandate to convert the world." From this perspective, attempting to install a fundamentalist, restrictive version of Christian faith into the US government is a logical, faithful task. But is that what Jesus had in mind? I no longer think this passage is a command to colonize the world for Christ. Instead, it is the culmination of a journey toward a more expansive and inclusive vision that is part of Matthew's Gospel. When Jesus encountered a Gentile woman who asked him to help her daughter in Matthew 15:22-28, he brushed her request off because she wasn't part of Israel. She was an outsider in need, but that need wasn't his mission or problem—until she responded with such faith that it stopped Jesus in his tracks and gave him a larger vision for his ministry.

In that light, I do not read Matthew 28 as communicating that we should force everyone to convert to our religion but a command from Jesus to open the doors of belonging. What if he's saying, "As you go into the world there will be others, people who don't look like you, believe like you, or practice like you, and they may want to join this movement. You will have the impulse that tells you to exclude them, but I am telling you to get out of their way. They are taking the space that God made them take at this table; don't try to stop them." How would our past, present, and future be different if we'd read this text in this way?

NATIONALISM: AMERICA FIRST, JESUS LAST

"America First" is a slogan, alongside "Make America Great Again," around which white Christian nationalists have rallied. These mantras are also not new. In some ways, the 2020s have eerie and unfortunate similarities with the 1920s and 30s, both in America and around the world. Those with ears to hear and eyes to see should be seriously alarmed.

Nationalism masquerades as just being concerned about one's own culture and country, but it's so much more than that.

In a country like America, a place that in the past has been proud of our diversity—that anyone in the world could come to the United States and be an American—nationalism is a direct attempt to create a homogeneous culture where people of European decent have power, control, and inherent belonging, and anyone not fitting that description is just lucky to be here.

Further, nationalism seeks to ignore and shirk the responsibility incumbent upon countries and people with power to use it for the well-being and flourishing of all people and countries. Nationalists seek to make America an isolated nation that only helps the world when it is convenient and beneficial to do so. The problem with this, of course, is that caring for others is rarely convenient and not always immediately beneficial to the one doing the caring. When we understand that we all inhabit the same planet, and that our fates are tied up together, the calculation changes. It doesn't matter if you are in first class, coach, or economy, if the plane goes down, everyone on board is in trouble. Nationalism misses that important truth about our shared existence—that it is, in fact, a shared existence.

How can this approach be justified when the call to care for the poor, forgotten, and marginalized comes again and again in the pages of Scripture? It's a "what you look for you will find" situation. There are absolutely texts in the Bible that are nationalistic in nature. For example, the short work of the prophet Obadiah focuses on how bad Edom is and how the God of Israel would give his people victory over the awful

Edomites. Yes, that vision of an us/them—God is for us and against them—is present in Scripture. But, thank God, so is the alternative. In Isaiah 25, the prophet envisions a world in which God has called all people to the same mountain, to a human unity, symbolized by a feast, that transcends the ways in which we divide ourselves:

> *On this mountain the* Lord *of hosts will make for all peoples*
> > *a feast of rich food, a feast of well-aged wines,*
> > *of rich food filled with marrow, of well-aged wines*
> > *strained clear.*
> *And he will destroy on this mountain*
> > *the shroud that is cast over all peoples,*
> > *the covering that is spread over all nations;*
> > *he will swallow up death forever.*
>
> > > > > *(Isaiah 25:6-8a)*

Perhaps the most powerful picture of God's longing to bring humanity together, instead of separation and isolation, is the story of Jonah. This short parable about a reluctant prophet who ran from God's call has captured our imagination, but I sometimes wonder if we have missed the challenge of it. It is not a story that threatens what God will do to us if we disobey orders but a call to see others, even our enemies, in the case of the Ninevites for Jonah, as worthy of God's love and our care. Toward the end of the story, as Jonah sulks about the fact that God didn't destroy Nineveh as he'd hoped, God gives Jonah a hard pill to swallow. Jonah is angry about a plant that died, a plant that he did not cultivate or tend to. God uses that experience as a teaching moment for the prophet.

> But God said to Jonah, "Is it right for you to be angry about the bush?" And he said, "Yes, angry enough to die." Then the LORD said, "You are concerned about the bush, for which you did not labor and which you did not grow; it came into being in a night and perished in a night. And should I not be concerned about Nineveh, that great city, in which there are more than a hundred and twenty thousand persons who do not know their right hand from their left and also many animals?"
>
> (Jonah 4:9-11)

Christian Nationalism fails to understand, to take seriously that God's love and care transcend our borders and our passports. It also fails to understand that God's love and care are not tied to our doctrinal positions or religious affiliation. God's love is too big, our fates are too connected for us to give in to the fear, bigotry, and violence of white Christian nationalism.

WHAT DO WE DO ABOUT WHITE CHRISTIAN NATIONALISM?

One of the responses I often see to Christian nationalism relies on what is often referred to as the "no true Scotsman" fallacy. To put it simply, we see this when someone suggests that Christian nationalists—or really any Christian or group of Christians that are behaving in ways that are frustrating and embarrassing to other Christians—aren't *real* Christians. This is an attempt to put distance between the person making this claim and those with whom they don't want to associate. To be honest, I completely understand the impulse. I don't like the fact that some Christians behave in very un-Christlike ways. It would be great to be able to redraw the boundary line, with them on the outside, but that's not how any of this works.

What makes someone a Christian is not that I say they are or that they adhere to a specific doctrinal or theological system. If that were the case, which one is the "correct" option? There are more than forty thousand Christian denominations, and we are to assume that one of them has it all figured out? One group managed to conquer mystery and the unknown? Highly unlikely, to the point of impossibility. Further, I am on the receiving end of the "you're not a real Christian" comments sometimes, but that doesn't mean I'm not. We just don't get to tell people who they are and how they identify. What we can do, however, is talk meaningfully about what *kind of Christians* we are.

When we waste time and energy attempting to move people out from under the label we are trying to protect, we fail to address the real problems. Some Christians behave in ways that are antithetical to the teachings and way of Jesus, and instead of trying to pretend they aren't part of our "us," we must address it head on. Jesus gave us a framework for such an important task. He told his followers—including us—that we can make decisions about the kind of faith with which we are dealing.

> *"Beware of false prophets, who come to you in sheep's clothing but inwardly are ravenous wolves. You will know them by their fruits. Are grapes gathered from thorns or figs from thistles? In the same way, every good tree bears good fruit, but the bad tree bears bad fruit. A good tree cannot bear bad fruit, nor can a bad tree bear good fruit. Every tree that does not bear good fruit will be cut down and thrown into the fire. Thus you will know them by their fruits."*

> (Matthew 7:15-20)

Contextually, Jesus is likely referring to those voices that would seek to instigate the kind of violent revolt and revolution that led to the cataclysmic war with Rome of 66–72 CE. However, the principle embedded here seems universally applicable. If we want to understand what kind of person and what kind of faith someone has, the question to ask isn't, What do you believe? but rather, What do you do? Holding and espousing a specific doctrinal belief isn't the metric. It requires little to simply affirm or give assent to an idea. What we really believe is discovered through what we do. Our actions are the loudest and most authentic expression of our convictions.

Our task, then, is to measure our actions against what is Christlike. When white Christian nationalists spew hate and bigotry, the stench of their rotten fruit makes it obvious that, while they might be Christian, the message and way of Jesus have not shaped their behavior. The way we salvage some dignity and decency for our faith tradition is by living out of the ethic and values that Jesus is referring to when he speaks about the kingdom of God. That contrast, between love, compassion, and mercy on the one hand, and fear, indifference, and hate on the other, presents two very different understandings of Jesus and the Christian faith.

In these dark and heavy days, we do not need Christians of good will and conscience arguing about how get to wear our label. That will not move the needle in any meaningful way. What we need are Christians who take Jesus so seriously, who love God, self, and neighbor so beautifully that the distinction becomes clear. We need Christians who will uphold the dignity and well-being of immigrants, regardless of their status, who will defend the rights of women, the LGBTQ+ community, and anyone else whose rights are being trampled on by those whose vision of America and their faith is just too small and too unimaginative. After all, the best critique we can offer of something bad is the living and practicing of something better. As we embody the expansive, inclusive vision of Jesus, a better way to be Christian will become visible to those around us.

In the end, this chapter of American history and this co-opting of Jesus that white Christian nationalism has engaged in will not age well. It already smells like spoiled milk. Our task—those of us who are being transformed by the love of God that we have experienced in Jesus—is to live a better story, to be the voice of conscience and compassion, and to call our Christian siblings to a more Christlike faith.

5

Racism

TELLING OURSELVES THE TRUTH

I will never forget exactly where I was at 10 p.m. on Tuesday, November 4, 2008. At that moment I was enjoying one of my favorite pastimes, watching the returns of a highly anticipated presidential election. Things were different almost twenty years ago, and while politics have always been contentious and cut-throat, there was a sense of norms and civility that sadly no longer seem to exist. This election was especially exciting because it seemed likely to lead to a significant moment in the history of our country and the presidency. It wasn't about partisanship, but about possibility. Barack Obama, then a senator from Illinois, was on track to become the first African American president of these United States. I sat glued to the news coverage of the results, the anticipation building with each state called.

Then, at just a little past 10 p.m., all of the West Coast states were called and the Associated Press officially declared Barack Obama the winner, outpacing his opponent, John McCain, with 365 electoral votes to 173 for McCain. It was a surreal moment, and I remember just being overwhelmed with a sense of gratitude and hope, which were the very values around which the president-elect had run his campaign. It was a watershed moment in the history of our country, to be sure, but also a moment that, looking back, revealed my ignorance. As the election was called I thought to myself, "We did it. We defeated racism in this country."

My goodness, how wrong I was. Clearly, I did not understand the complexity and embeddedness of racism in the United States. Almost twenty years later, my proclamation has not aged well at all. In the decades since that moment, we've witnessed what some have called a "whitelash." In response to the election of President Obama, some had their worst ideas and perspectives deepened and reenergized, eventually spilling out on our televisions, social media, and everyday lives. The failure of elected leaders to denounce and condemn this growing expression of prejudice, bigotry, and hatred, for fear of being at odds with Donald Trump, has emboldened many white supremacists. In my own city of Nashville, we experienced literal Nazis marching in the streets. It is sobering and terrifying how similar the 2020s seem to the 1920s.

In short, I was wrong. We haven't solved our racism issues in the United States. Unfortunately, it seems some days that we are going in the opposite direction. This leads me to offer an acknowledgment and a disclaimer before we go any further in this discussion. I am a straight white male. That is the reality of my existence, and it comes with a kind of privilege that can prevent a person from seeing how things actually are. We have a tendency to not see what we've been taught not to look for, don't we? That has been my journey. I also recognize that racism and white supremacy, as we will see, are baked into the crust of America. That fact can make us feel defensive, I know. After all, none of us wants to be considered to be racist, especially if we are working to disentangle ourselves from that way of being. That is good and holy work, and we must keep doing it. However, it is also true that when we've been swimming in the ocean, we can't avoid getting wet. That's what I learned after election night in 2008, that America has a racism and white supremacy problem that is deeply intertwined with our origins, and our refusal to really deal with the roots of racism has limited our ability to exorcise that demon. Defensiveness will only stifle our progress and growth. Racism is a system, not just an individual prejudice or bigotry. People can be racist, even unknowingly, but that is the result of a system that has been set up to perpetuate that injustice.

One brief example of this. I grew up in the South, in Appalachia. Our family would never have considered ourselves to be racist. How could we be? We had dear friends who were not white, and that, to us, meant that we surely could not have a racist bone in our bodies. Looking back, I can remember specific phrases—sayings that were common in our conversations—that I now know are horribly demeaning and racist. We lived in the very cradle of American racism; it was woven into the fabric of our lives. Of course, we were formed and shaped by it, even if unwittingly and unintentionally. Untangling ourselves from that experience is like trying to undo a tangled mess of Christmas lights. It does not happen overnight, and it takes actual work. It requires that we tell ourselves the truth—the truth about our country, its founding, and the source of our abundance—and that might make us uncomfortable. Yes, the truth will set us free, but at first it might make us miserable.

THE ORIGINS OF RACISM
IN AMERICA

When I first began learning about the history of racism, I was shocked to discover that it is not nearly as old as you might imagine. In fact, before the sixteenth century the word race simply referred to people who shared a relational origin or group connection of some sort. For example, we might talk about "the human race." However, in the 1500s a new meaning for race was introduced that focused on categorizing people into social groups based on shared characteristics—like skin color—and using that designation to either extend or deny certain benefits or privileges. To put it succinctly, race is not a biological fact but a human construct. We made up the idea of race in order to have justification for denying certain groups their rights. Well, those of us that share European descent, anyway. Race and racism were the product of the project of colonialism. As we saw in the previous chapter, as explorers set out to discover new lands, they did so with divine permission, supplied by the popes, to take whatever they wanted and to enslave Indigenous populations in the name of Christ. In order to do that, they needed to create a narrative that depicted the people they were so brutally killing and subjugating as somehow deficient or less than, thus deserving what they were getting. In turn, they would seek to convert their victims and celebrate just how benevolent they were in bringing Christ to the lost. It was all just a pretext, an excuse to justify their brutality.

This means that while race is a relatively new idea in human history, it is all America has ever known. David R. Roediger, the professor of American studies at the University of Kansas, puts it this way: "The world got along without race for the overwhelming majority of its history. The US has never been without it."[1]

This is why we must acknowledge that to be an American is to live and exist in a system that has known and perpetuated racism since day one. It is not the claim that all Americans are horrible racists but that we are all raised in a system that is founded in racism. Our resistance to the acknowledgment of that truth is significantly hampering the work to change that reality. In our current era, instead of teaching our children the truth of our founding and history—of our treatment of the Indigenous peoples of North America, slavery, segregation, and so on—in age-appropriate ways, many of our leaders are trying to completely remove any lessons that might make white kids uncomfortable. Instead, there is movement that seeks to sanitize and reshape the American story in ways that will only perpetuate a past we can't outrun. Racism, and its attendant white supremacy, is America's original sin, and as with any sin, we cannot be free from its power and control until we name it, repent of it, and seek to live differently. Like Zacchaeus, whose encounter with Jesus changed his way of seeing and being, we need a radical change that allows us to confront our history in order to chart a better future for equality and equity for all Americans.

SHOW ME THE MONEY

At the core of racism is also greed. Racism was the mechanism through which the project of colonialism achieved success. Deeming a specific group as less than, somehow not quite as human as we are, gave cover for the inhumane system of the Atlantic slave trade. Racism wasn't just born as a prejudice, but as a way to achieve economic abundance with as little overhead as possible. When your labor force is not compensated, when they count toward your net worth, you can make a lot of money without a lot of cost. In fact, one of the arguments used in the Southern states prior to and during the American Civil War is that abolishing slavery would crash the economy. Let that sink in for just a minute. Some of our ancestors saw other humans as sources of profit that did not deserve basic human rights, and the attempt to extend those rights to others who deserved them was seen as an economic attack.

This is also why the fact that we, as a country, have never enacted any kind of reparations is immoral. When enslaved people were liberated, they were not given compensation for their years of labor, nor were they given land on which to live and create their own wealth. The owners of enslaved people, however, were compensated. On April 16, 1862, a little more than eight months before he issued the Emancipation Proclamation, President Abraham Lincoln signed a bill that ended slavery in Washington, DC. That bill awarded the owners of enslaved people who were pro-Union up to $300 for each person freed. Today that would equate to just under $10,000. The District of Columbia Emancipation Act freed enslaved people, but it did not compensate them; it compensated those who had claimed ownership over them and benefited from their free labor. But that labor was not free, was it? It had a significant human cost, a cost we still have not reckoned with to this day.

THE CHRISTIAN ROOTS
OF RACISM

As much as we may not like it, the roots of racism in America are intertwined with the Christian tradition. The explorers who discovered the New World were understood to have a divine mandate to claim these new-to-them lands and their inhabitants under the guise of spreading the footprint of the Christian faith in the world. They were not just explorers; they were Christian explorers. As such, eventually, they needed some kind of biblical justification to support their actions. There's a verse for everything if we want it badly enough, isn't there? The Bible, for the first time, was then weaponized to justify the racism that upheld the system that was benefiting the powerful.

In the account of the Exodus, a brand new idea entered our human story. In the ancient world, and even today, there is a tendency to view those with wealth and power as being divinely supported. God, they thought then, as some do now, was on the side of those with all the money and all the control. How else would they have these things? The story of the Exodus turns that narrative on its head. This God, the God of Moses, was not the defender of the powerful but upholds the cause of the powerless. This God doesn't prop up kings; this God liberates the enslaved. It was a radical new idea.

Yet texts from that same library were used to justify racism and uphold the enslavement of other humans, and those texts were interpreted to be more binding than the texts of liberation. Condoning slavery wasn't enough though. There needed to be a justification for enslaving this particular group of people. They needed God to be against people with black and brown skin. It only took four chapters into the Bible to get there. Again, we find what we look for, and if we don't, we invent it.

In Genesis 4, after Cain has committed the first murder, killing his brother, Abel, God announces to Cain the consequences of his action. Cain will be sent away. Notice the exchange between them:

> Now you are cursed from the ground, which has opened its mouth to receive your brother's blood from your hand. When you till the ground, it will no longer yield to you its strength; you will be a fugitive and a wanderer on the earth." Cain said to the LORD, "My punishment is greater than I can bear! Today you have driven me away from the soil, and I shall be hidden from your face; I shall be a fugitive and a wanderer on the earth, and anyone who meets me may kill me." Then the LORD said to him, "Not so! Whoever kills Cain will suffer a sevenfold vengeance." And the LORD put a mark on Cain, so that no one who came upon him would kill him. Then Cain went away from the presence of the LORD and settled in the land of Nod, east of Eden.
>
> (Genesis 4:11-16)

When readers looking for a text to support the enslavement of Africans came to this passage and read about the "mark of Cain," they knew what it meant. The mark of Cain, they said, was having black skin. So, by enslaving people with black skin, they were just upholding God's curse of Cain in the Bible. A similar interpretive scenario played out with the "curse of Ham" in Genesis 9. These texts were weaponized as prooftexts to defend the indefensible.

I am not saying "only Christians can be racist." Of course that is not true. What I am saying is that the origins of racism, particularly in America, are Christian, which means Christians like you and me have an obligation to address it and to work to dismantle the white supremacy that is so deeply ingrained in our systems.

WHAT DO WE DO NOW?

The point of this chapter is not to just heap guilt upon white people for the evils our ancestors perpetrated. We do, however, bear responsibility to change things, to move toward justice and equity in meaningful ways. While I do not have access to a time machine, the future is still unfolding before us. The past is beyond our reach, but the present and future can be transformed by both our inaction and our action. This responsibility we bear has both personal and political implications. Individual and communal responses are needed.

Let's begin with the personal. We have, as Americans, a responsibility to acknowledge how the system of racism has impacted and formed each of us. This is especially true for people who are white, like me. As we witness an attack on equality right before our eyes through the dismantling of DEI programs and initiatives and the rollback of checks and balances that prevent discrimination, like affirmative action, it is all the more important that we step up and step in to this work. This acknowledgment, for me as a white person, doesn't mean I haven't worked hard in my life. It simply means that others have, too, and that in this system we have inherited, the hard work of people who look like me has counted for more than the hard work of others who don't occupy my space of privilege. It does not demean what I have done or belittle that work. It does, however, acknowledge that in our system the hard work of Black, Indigenous, and other people of color (BIPOC) isn't always as valued, and the avenues for opportunity aren't as accessible. That is not a condemnation of me or you but the system. At the same time, when we defend the system, then we do become complicit. Acknowledgment is an important first step, but it is not the only work.

We are also called to dismantle these unjust systems that uphold racism and white supremacy. That will no doubt require a lot of work, and it begins with a commitment to being anti-racist. Anti-racism refers to the intentional practice of opposing racism and working toward equity and justice. There are several first steps on this journey that can be helpful.

First, we must actively seek out education. Taking courses and trainings on anti-racism and implicit bias are a good first step. My wife and I were foster parents in the past. That's how all of our kids came into our lives, and I can't even begin to express what a gift they are. Part of being an active foster parent home means keeping up with a certain amount of training hours per year. Look, I'll be honest here. Some of those trainings were about as fun as watching paint dry. However, one particular training around implicit bias left an indelible mark on me. That two-hour training was one of the most illuminating educational experiences of my life. It helped me see that, of course, I obviously have ingrained and implicit biases I am not even aware of and gave me the invitation to name them and become aware of them. Perhaps this could look like a church or small group seeking out educational resources or experts that can introduce this important work and offer guidance on the way. This is an indispensable first step.

Another practice that can be meaningful is to hold those around us, and ourselves, accountable for our words and actions. Are you ever in a situation in which someone, maybe even me or you, says or does something that upholds the system of racism? We shouldn't be surprised, should we? It's the system in which we've been immersed, after all. What do we do in those situations? We can just ignore it, telling ourselves we are keeping the peace, sure. But a peace predicated on ignoring injustice and not talking about things that matter is no peace at all. We don't need to jump into attack mode or use shame as a tool to make people or ourselves feel bad. Instead, we can lean in with curiosity, acknowledging what was said or done and placing the action in conversation. The goal, after all, is not to shame or call out, but to call in to a better, more just way to be human. I have found something like, "I know you might not have meant it this way, but it can be really harmful," is a good way to engage. Also, acknowledging the ways we have found ourselves in a similar situation can be inviting.

Engaging at a larger level is also essential. That may look like writing letters to our elected officials, attending organizing events and protests, and taking other opportunities to use our voices and influence to dismantle the injustices and inequities that we see.

Shame and guilt, which are often the first uninvited guests to arrive in these conversations, are the great limiters of our progress as individuals and as a country. It is far more helpful to show up with humility, compassion, and grace, for ourselves and for others. When we know we have a lot to learn and a long way to go, there is no shame or guilt. There is just opportunity. I have never gotten anything totally, perfectly right. I am a work in progress, and I bet you are too. Our job is to keep showing up, to keep being open and humble, to keep learning, and to keep God's dream for a world of justice and equity at the center of all of our work. Then, one day, as we keep pushing forward, our actions will "let justice roll down like water and righteousness like an ever-flowing stream" (Amos 5:24).

That version of me back in 2008 had good intentions. He was just woefully ill-informed. I'm sure this version of me has plenty to learn too. The key is to keep showing up in humility and to be willing to do the hard work that is before us.

Postscript

In every courtroom drama there is a moment of significant tension. After the prosecution and defense present their respective cases, cross-examine the witnesses, and exhaust the evidence available, they rest. Then the jury must decide. In this little volume I have offered interpretations of key topics that will shape the future of Christianity for better or for worse. Through these interpretations we have explored the roots, both in history and the text, and asked if our inherited understandings have served us well. This book by no means is the last word. It is the first word, the beginning of a conversation. My hope is that you will engage in meaningful deliberation with those with whom you are on the journey.

In my work as a pastor, I often encounter people who have a conflicted relationship with the Bible and Christianity, many for reasons that can be found in the contents of this book. They have been on the receiving end of a weaponized Bible. They have been told that their gender or sexual orientation limits their belonging and participation. They have experienced racism, justified by chapter and verse. And they have watched as white Christian nationalism seeks to remove the rights and opportunities that are available to them and those they love. So often, people have been led to believe that they must choose between being what they believe is a good human being or being faithful to the Bible, their faith, and, ultimately, God. I hope this cross-examination has opened the door for us to see that the interpretations we have inherited aren't the only options, and sometimes they aren't even the best option. Our choice is not between abandoning the Bible or ignoring the issues that matter to us. The goal is to take the Bible seriously as an ancient library that contains the experiences, interpretations, and dreams of our spiritual ancestors. Then we can begin to discover how the Bible, theology, and faith can be an unfolding process that is still meaningful and helpful today.

I rest my case.

Notes

2. Gender Equality

1   Thomas Cahill, *Desire of the Everlasting Hills: The World Before and After Jesus* (New York: Doubleday, 1999), 147.

4. White Christian Nationalism

1   Brian Kaylor and Beau Underwood, "The Prayers of January 6," Wordandway.org, *A Public Witness*, January 6, 2022, https://publicwitness.wordandway.org/p/the-prayers-of-january-6.

2   Quoted from John Francis Maxwell, *Slavery and the Catholic Church: The History of Catholic Teaching Concerning the Moral Legitimacy of the Institution of Slavery* (London: Barry Rose, 1975), 53.

5. Racism

1   David R. Roediger, *How Race Survived US History: From Settlement and Slavery to the Obama Phenomenon* (New York: Verso, 2008), xii.